1.25 ʼNI

TIME FOR REFLECTION

Edited by

LOUISE BACHELDER

with illustrations by

PAT STEWART

———

PETER PAUPER PRESS
Mount Vernon, New York

ON THE NEED FOR A REST

There is no music in a "rest," but there is the making of music in it. In our whole life melody, the music is broken off here and there by "rests," and we foolishly think we have come to the end of the tune. God sends a time of forced leisure — sickness, disappointed plans, frustrated efforts — and makes a sudden pause in the choral hymn of our lives, and we lament that our voices must be silent and our part missing in the music which ever goes up to the ear of the Creator. How does the musician read the "rest"? See him beat time with unvarying count and catch up the next note true and steady as if no breaking place had come in between. Not without design does God write the music of our lives. But be it ours to learn the time and not be dismayed at the "rests." They are not to be slurred, not to be omitted, not to destroy the melody, nor to change the keynote. If we look up, God Himself will beat the time for us. With the eye on Him we shall strike the next note full and clear.

JOHN RUSKIN

TIME FOR REFLECTION

WHAT sunshine is to flowers, smiles are to humanity. They are but trifles to be sure; but, scattered along life's pathway, the good they do is inconceivable.

JOSEPH ADDISON

SOME people are always grumbling because roses have thorns. I am thankful that thorns have roses.

ALPHONSE KARR

THE LORD is good; his mercy is everlasting.
PSALMS 100:5

THE three primary principles of wisdom: obedience to the laws of God, concern for the welfare of mankind, and suffering with fortitude all the accidents of life.

ANONYMOUS

THE more we live by our intellect, the less we understand the meaning of life.

WILLIAM JAMES

A BOOK is a garden, an orchard, a storehouse, a party, a company by the way, a counsellor, a multitude of counsellors.

HENRY WARD BEECHER

ALWAYS remember to forget
The troubles that passed away,
But never forget to remember
The blessings that come each day.

ANONYMOUS

POLITENESS to superiors is duty — to equals courtesy — to inferiors nobleness.

BENJAMIN FRANKLIN

THE sun rises when morning comes, the mist rises from the meadow, the dew rises from the clover; but oh, when will my heart arise?

WELSH (TRADITIONAL)

ALL the darkness of the world cannot put out the light of one small candle.

ANONYMOUS

As surgeons keep their instruments and knives always at hand for cases requiring immediate treatment, so shouldst thou have thy thoughts ready to understand things divine and human, remembering in thy every act, even the smallest, how close is the bond that unites the two.

MARCUS AURELIUS

THE first and best victory is to conquer self; to be conquered by self is, of all things, the most shameful and vile.

PLATO

SURE, He that made us with such large
   discourse,
Looking before and after, gave us not
That capability and god-like reason
To fust in us unused. . . .

WILLIAM SHAKESPEARE

MERE life is not a blessing, but to live well.

SENECA

TRUTH above all, even when it upsets and overwhelms us.

HENRI-FRÉDÉRIC AMIEL

CHEERFULNESS means a contented spirit, a pure heart, a kind and loving disposition; it means humility and charity, a generous appreciation of others, and a modest opinion of self.

WILLIAM MAKEPEACE THACKERAY

THOUGH we travel the world over to find the beautiful, we must carry it with us or we find it not.

ANONYMOUS

No longer forward nor behind I look in hope
    or fear;
But grateful, take the good I find, the
    best of now and here.

JOHN GREENLEAF WHITTIER

GREAT God, I ask thee for no meaner pelf
Than that I may not disappoint myself,
That in my action I may soar as high
As I can now discern with this clear eye.

HENRY DAVID THOREAU

BY a tranquil mind, I mean nothing else than a mind well ordered.

MARCUS AURELIUS

WE receive everything, both life and happiness; but the *manner* in which we receive, this is what is still ours. Let us, then, receive trustfully without shame or anxiety. Let us humbly accept from God even our own nature, and treat it charitably, firmly, intelligently. Not that we are called upon to accept the evil and the disease in us, but let us accept *ourselves* in spite of the evil and the disease.

HENRI-FRÉDÉRIC AMIEL

APPREHENSIONS are God's introductions extended inscrutably.

EMILY DICKINSON

HAST never come to thee an hour,
A sudden gleam divine, precipitating,
    bursting all these bubbles, fashions,
    wealth?
These eager business aims — books, politics,
    art, amours,
To utter nothingness?

WALT WHITMAN

THE eternal God is thy refuge, and underneath are the everlasting arms.

DEUTERONOMY 33:27

ALL higher motives, ideals, conceptions, sentiments in a man are of no account if they do not come forward to strengthen him for the better discharge of the duties which devolve upon him in the ordinary affairs of life.

HENRY WARD BEECHER

USE well the moment; what the hour
Brings for thy use is in thy power;
And what thou best canst understand
Is just the thing lies nearest to thy hand.

JOHANN WOLFGANG VON GOETHE

THE essence of humour is sensibility; warm tender fellow-feeling with all forms of existence.

THOMAS CARLYLE

PRAYER is the little implement
Through which men reach
Where presence is denied them.

EMILY DICKINSON

WHEN thou liest down, thou shalt not be afraid: yea, thou shalt lie down, and thy sleep shall be sweet.

PROVERBS 3:24

THE most disastrous times have produced the greatest minds. The purest metal comes of the most ardent furnace, the most brilliant lightning comes of the darkest clouds.

FRANÇOIS RENÉ DE CHATEAUBRIAND

TRY first thyself, and after call in God;
For to the worker God himself lends aid.

EURIPIDES

COMPASSION is the chief law of human existence.

FYODOR DOSTOEVSKY

LOVE is the life of man.

EMANUEL SWEDENBORG

WITHOUT hearts there is no home.

LORD GEORGE NOEL GORDON BYRON

GOD keeps His holy mysteries
Just on the outside of man's dream.

ELIZABETH BARRETT BROWNING

A HERO is one who knows how to hang on one minute longer.

ANONYMOUS

IT is with life as with a play — it matters not how long the action is spun out, but how good the acting is.

SENECA

GOD enters by a private door into every individual.

RALPH WALDO EMERSON

HE that can have patience can have what he will.

BENJAMIN FRANKLIN

GENIUS is eternal patience.

MICHAELANGELO

FOR everything exists and not one sigh
   nor smile nor tear,
One hair nor particle of dust, not one
   can pass away.

WILLIAM BLAKE

WHEN I am attacked by gloomy thoughts, nothing helps me so much as running to my books. They quickly absorb me and banish the clouds from my mind.

MIGUEL DE MONTAIGNE

MORE helpful than all wisdom or counsel is one draught of simple human pity that will not forsake us.

GEORGE ELIOT

SORROW is a fruit: God does not make it grow on limbs too weak to bear it.

VICTOR HUGO

WITH most people lovability is not absent — it is merely undiscovered.

ANONYMOUS

THE great thing in the world is not so much where we stand, as in what direction we are moving.

OLIVER WENDELL HOLMES

A GRINDSTONE that had not grit in it, how long would it take to sharpen an axe? And affairs that had not grit in them, how long would they take to make a man?

HENRY WARD BEECHER

CHEERFULNESS is the best promoter of health, and is as friendly to the mind as to the body.

JOSEPH ADDISON

CERTAINLY, in our own little sphere it is not the most active people to whom we owe the most. Among the common people whom we know, it is not necessarily those who are busiest, not those who, meteor-like, are ever on the rush after some visible charge and work. It is the lives, like the stars, which simply pour down on us the calm light of their bright and faithful being, up to which we look and out of which we gather the deepest calm and courage. It seems to me that there is reassurance here for many of us who seem to have no chance for active usefulness. We can do nothing for our fellow-men. But still it is good to know that we can be something for them; to know (and this we may know surely) that no man or woman of the humblest sort can really be strong, gentle, pure, and good, without the world being better for it, without somebody being helped and comforted by the very existence of that goodness.

PHILLIPS BROOKS

I KNOW that This World is a World of Imagination and Vision.

WILLIAM BLAKE

15

Sweet are the uses of adversity;
Which, like the toad, ugly and venomous,
Wears yet a precious jewel in his head;
And this our life, exempt from public haunt,
Finds tongues in trees, books in the running
    brooks,
Sermons in stones, and good in everything.
I would not change it.

                    WILLIAM SHAKESPEARE

A word fitly spoken is like apples of gold in
pictures of silver.

                    PROVERBS 25:11

What do we live for; if it is not to make life
less difficult to each other?

                    GEORGE ELIOT

I am an old man and have known a great
many troubles, but most of them never hap-
pened.

                    MARK TWAIN

True friends visit us in prosperity only when
invited, but in adversity they come without
invitation.

                    THEOPHRASTUS

Do not pray for easy lives. Pray to be stronger men! Do not pray for tasks equal to your powers. Pray for powers equal to your tasks.

PHILLIPS BROOKS

To the man who himself strives earnestly, God also lends a helping hand.

AESCHYLUS

NOT in the clamor of the crowded street, Not in the shouts and plaudits of the throng, But in ourselves are triumph and defeat.

HENRY WADSWORTH LONGFELLOW

WHAT we obtain too cheap we esteem too lightly; 'tis dearness only that gives everything its value.

THOMAS PAINE

NOTHING is so strong as gentleness, Nothing is so gentle as real strength.

ST. FRANCIS DE SALES

HE is a wise man who does not grieve for the things which he has not, but rejoices for those which he has.

EPICTETUS

He hath said, I will never leave thee, nor forsake thee.

HEBREWS 13:5

Out of the night that covers me,
  Black as the pit from pole to pole,
I thank whatever gods may be
  For my unconquerable soul.

In the fell clutch of Circumstance
  I have not winced nor cried aloud;
Under the bludgeonings of Chance
  My head is bloody, but unbow'd.

          . . . . . .

It matters not how straight the gate,
  How charged with punishment the scroll,
I am the master of my fate;
  I am the captain of my soul.

WILLIAM ERNEST HENLEY

We must always change, renew, rejuvenate
ourselves; otherwise we harden.

JOHANN WOLFGANG VON GOETHE

Nothing happens to any man which he is
not formed by nature to bear.

MARCUS AURELIUS

MAKE peace with yourself, and heaven and earth will make peace with you. Endeavour to enter your own inner cell, and you will see the heavens; because the one and the other are one and the same, and when you enter one you see the two.

ST. ISAAK OF SYRIA

No one truly knows happiness who has not suffered, and the redeemed are happier than the elect.

HENRI-FRÉDÉRIC AMIEL

FIRE is the test of gold; adversity, of strong men.

SENECA

Do good with what thou hast, or it will do thee no good.

WILLIAM PENN

SORROWS are often like clouds which, though black when they are passing over us, when they are past, become as if they were garments of God, thrown off in purple and gold along the sky.

HENRY WARD BEECHER

For we are saved by hope: but hope that is seen is not hope: for what a man seeth, why doth he yet hope for?

But if we hope for that we see not, *then* do we with patience wait for *it*.

Romans 8:24, 25

But God is not like human-kind;
Man cannot read the Almighty mind;
Vengeance will never torture thee,
Nor hunt thy soul eternally.

Then do not in this night of grief,
This time of overwhelming fear,
O do not think that God can leave,
Forget, forsake, refuse to hear!

Emily Brontë

They that sow in tears shall reap in joy.

Psalms 126:5

Wisdom is to the soul what health is to the body.

François, Duc de la Rochefoucauld

Sympathy gives us the material for wisdom.

Anonymous

THERE is no remembrance more blessed, and nothing more blessed to remember, than suffering overcome in solidarity with God; this is the mystery of suffering.

SOREN AABYE KIERKEGAARD

DEAR Lord, let me recount to Thee
Some of the great things Thou has done
    For me, even me,
    Thy little one.

CHRISTINA ROSETTI

I BELIEVE in the human being, mind and flesh; form and soul.

RICHARD JEFFERIES

THERE is some soul of goodness in things evil,
Would men observingly distil it out . . .
Thus may we gather honey from the weed,
And make a moral of the devil himself.

WILLIAM SHAKESPEARE

GOD is . . . even in the depths of Hell.

WILLIAM BLAKE

ONE ought not to desire the impossible.

LEONARDO DA VINCI

MAY the road rise to meet you. May the wind be always at your back. May the sun shine warm upon your face, the rains fall soft upon your fields and, until we meet again, may God hold you in the palm of His Hand.

IRISH PRAYER

To breathe is a beatitude.

HENRI-FRÉDÉRIC AMIEL

YOU, little child, with your shining eyes and dimpled cheeks — you can lead us along the pathway to the more abundant life:

WE blundering grownups need in our lives the virtues that you have in yours:

THE tolerance that forgets differences as quickly as your childish quarrels are spent; that holds no grudges, that hates never, that loves people for what they are:

THE genuineness of being oneself; to be done with sham, pretense and empty show; to be simple, natural, and sincere:

THE courage that rises from defeat and tries again, as you with laughing face rebuild the house of blocks that topples to the floor:

The believing heart that trusts others, knows no fear and has faith in a Divine Father who watches over His children from the sky:

The continued, trusting mind that, at the close of day, woos the blessing of child-like slumber:

Little child, we would become like you, that we may find again the Kingdom of Heaven within our hearts.

ANONYMOUS

GRATITUDE is heaven itself.

WILLIAM BLAKE

LIFE is mostly froth and bubble;
    Two things stand like stone:
Kindness in another's trouble,
    Courage in your own.

ADAM LINDSAY GORDON

NOR can we fall below the arms of God, how low soever it be we fall.

WILLIAM PENN

ANYONE that suffers is God's representative.

VIVEKANANDA

Whatsoever things are true, whatsoever things are honest, whatsoever things are just, whatsoever things are pure, whatsoever things are lovely, whatsoever things are of good report; if there be any virtue, and if there be any praise, think on these things.

Philippians 4:8

. . . and thence we know
That Man subsists by Brotherhood and
    Universal Love.
We fall on one another's necks, more closely
    we embrace.
Not for ourselves, but for the Eternal family
    we live.
Man liveth not by Self alone, but in his
    brother's face
Each shall behold the Eternal Father and love
    and joy abound.

William Blake

It is a good and safe rule to sojourn in every place, as if you meant to spend your life there, never omitting an opportunity of doing a kindness, or speaking a true word, or making a friend.

John Ruskin

LET me have wider feelings, more extended sympathies; let me feel with all living things, rejoice and praise with them. Let me have deeper knowledge, a nearer insight, a more reverent conception. . . . Expand the mind until it grasps the idea of the unseen forces which hold the globe suspended and draw the vast suns and stars through space. Let it see the life, the organisms which dwell in those great worlds, and feel with them their hopes and joys and sorrows. Ever upwards, onwards, wider, deeper, broader, till capable of all.

How grand and holy is this life! How sacred the temple which contains it.

RICHARD JEFFERIES

A MERRY heart doeth good like a medicine.

PROVERBS 17:22

THEY also serve who only stand and wait.

JOHN MILTON

CAST all your care on God! That anchor holds.

ALFRED, LORD TENNYSON

A KNOWLEDGE that another has felt as we have felt, and seen things not much otherwise than we have seen them, will continue to the end to be one of life's choicest blessings.

ROBERT LOUIS STEVENSON

... ALL who joy would win
Must share it, — Happiness was born a twin.

LORD GEORGE NOEL GORDON BYRON

A LITTLE love, a little trust,
    A soft impulse, a sudden dream —
And life as dry as desert dust
    Is fresher than a mountain stream.

STOPFORD A. BROOKE

IT is impossible for that man to despair who remembers that his Helper is omnipotent.

JEREMY TAYLOR

No man will speak long with any interest, when he thinks about himself.

HENRY WARD BEECHER

To everything there is a season, and a time to every purpose under the heaven.

ECCLESIASTES 3:1

BE patient with every one, but above all with yourself. I mean, do not be disturbed because of your imperfections, and always rise up bravely from a fall.

ST. FRANCIS DE SALES

ANOTHER flower shall spring, because the soul of sweet delight can never pass away.

WILLIAM BLAKE

THE LORD is nigh unto all them that call upon Him.

PSALMS 145:18

MUCH drawback! what were earth
    without?
Is this our ultimate stage, or starting place
To try man's foot, if it will creep or climb,
'Mid obstacles in seeming, points that prove
Advantage for who vaults from low to high,
And makes the stumbling block a
    stepping-stone.

ROBERT BROWNING

Lo, I am with you alway, even unto the end of the world.

ST. MATTHEW 28:20

WHEN we are unhurried and wise, we perceive that only great and worthy things have any permanent and absolute existence — that petty fears and petty pleasures are but the shadow of reality.

HENRY DAVID THOREAU

FAIN would I hold my lamp aloft,
Like yonder tower built high above the reef,
Steadfast, tho' tempests rave or winds blow
    soft,
Clear, tho' the sky dissolve in tears of grief.
For darkness passes; storms shall not abide.
A little patience, and the fog is past,
After the sorrow of the ebbing tide,
The singing flood returns in joy at last.
The night is long, and pain weighs heavily;
But God will hold His world above despair.
Look to the east, where up the lucid sky
The morning climbs! The day shall yet be
    fair!

CELIA THAXTER

WE must learn to reawaken and keep ourselves awake, not by mechanical aids, but by an infinite expectation of the dawn.

HENRY DAVID THOREAU

It is more blessed to give than to receive; yet
a noble nature can accept and be thankful.

JOHANN AUGUST STRINDBERG

THE prayer of one pure heart, I think, hath
might to atone for many.

SOPHOCLES

THE more we know, the better we forgive;
Whoe'er feels deeply, feels for all who live.

MADAME DE STAËL

FOR the things that are seen are Temporal:
but the things that are not seen are Eternal.

JOHN BUNYAN

WHAT else is Wisdom? What of man's
    endeavour
Or God's high grace so lovely and so great?
To stand from fear set free, to breathe
    and wait.

EURIPIDES

COURAGE and perseverance have a magical
talisman, before which difficulties disappear
and obstacles vanish into air.

JOHN QUINCY ADAMS

THE first duty for a man is still that of subduing *Fear*. We must get rid of *Fear;* we cannot act at all till then. A man's acts are slavish, not true but specious; his very thoughts are false, he thinks as a slave and coward, till he has got *Fear* under his feet. A man shall and must be valiant; he must march forward, and quit himself like a man — trusting imperturbably in the appointment and *choice* of the upper Powers; and, on the whole, not fear at all. Now and always, the completeness of his victory over Fear will determine how much of a man he is.

THOMAS CARLYLE

ENJOY the blessings of this day, if God sends them; and the evils of it bear patiently and sweetly; for this day only is ours; we are dead to yesterday, and we are not yet born to the morrow.

JEREMY TAYLOR

EVERY man casts a shadow; not his body only, but his imperfectly mingled spirit. This is his grief. Let him turn which way he will, it falls opposite to the sun; short at noon, long at eve.

HENRY DAVID THOREAU

LAUGHTER, while it lasts, slackens and un-braces the mind, weakens the faculties, and causes a kind of remissness and dissolution in all the powers of the soul; and thus far it may be looked upon as a weakness in the composition of human nature. But if we consider the frequent reliefs we receive from it, and how often it breaks the gloom which is apt to depress the mind and damp our spirits, with transient, unexpected gleams of joy, one would take care not to grow too wise for so great a pleasure of life.

JOSEPH ADDISON

O MAGIC sleep! O comfortable bird
That broodest o'er the troubled sea of the
　　mind
Till it is hushed and smooth.

JOHN KEATS

'TIS the mind that makes the body rich.

WILLIAM SHAKESPEARE

THE mind is rarely so disturbed, but that the company of a friend will restore it to some degree of tranquility and sedateness.

ADAM SMITH

GOD's love for poor sinners is very wonder-
ful, but God's patience with ill-natured saints
is a deeper mystery.

HENRY DRUMMOND

WE live in deeds, not years;
In thoughts, not breath;
In feelings, not in figures on the dial.

We should count time
By heart-throbs when they beat
For God, for man, for duty.

He most lives
Who thinks most,
Feels noblest, acts the best.

PHILIP JAMES BAILEY

THE greatest man is he who chooses the right
with the most invincible resolution; who re-
sists the sorest temptation from within and
without; who bears the heaviest burden
cheerfully; who is calmest in storms, and
most fearless under menaces and frowns;
whose reliance on truth, on virtue, and on
God is most unfaltering.

SENECA

WISDOM will never let us stand with any man or men on unfriendly footing. We refuse sympathy and intimacy with people, as if we waited for some better sympathy or intimacy to come. But whence and when? Tomorrow will be like today. Life wastes itself whilst we are preparing to live.

RALPH WALDO EMERSON

AND the night shall be filled with music,
    And the cares that infest the day
Shall fold their tents like the Arabs,
    And as silently steal away.

HENRY WADSWORTH LONGFELLOW

THERE is a certain joy in weeping, for by tears grief is sated and relieved.

OVID

VICES and sins are a deadly poison; but virtues and good works are a healing medicine.

ST. FRANCIS OF ASSISI

THERE is no ill which may not be dissipated, like the dark, if you let in a stronger light upon it.

HENRY DAVID THOREAU

NOTHING is so soon forgot as pain. The moment it is gone the whole agony is over, and the thought of it can no longer give us any sort of disturbance.

ADAM SMITH

BE not ashamed to be helped; for it is thy business to do thy duty like a soldier in the assault on a town. How then, if being lame thou canst not mount up the battlements alone, but with the help of another it is possible?

MARCUS AURELIUS

NOTHING will ever be attempted if all possible objections must be first overcome.

SAMUEL JOHNSON

TEACH me to feel another's woe,
    To hide the fault I see;
That mercy I to others show,
    That mercy show to me.

ALEXANDER POPE

THE day is immeasurably long to him who knows not how to value and use it.

JOHANN WOLFGANG VON GOETHE

Do-nothing days may be the busiest ones. They are the days in which we absorb; while on the do-much days we try to make others absorb from us whatever we have in over-plus: ribbons, wisdom or cheese. If we of-tener eased the strain on our eyes and minds, we should be enriched by impressions that in our usual attent and mastering attitude we refuse to heed.

CHARLES M. SKINNER

It is no very severe reproach to any person that he does not possess heroic fortitude.

THOMAS MACAULAY

When love and skill work together, expect a masterpiece.

JOHN RUSKIN

He is the rich man, and enjoys the fruits of riches, who summer and winter forever can find delight in his own thoughts.

HENRY DAVID THOREAU

Of the blessings set before you, make your choice and be content.

SAMUEL JOHNSON

However mean your life is, meet it and live it; do not shun it and call it hard names. It is not so bad as you are. It looks poorest when you are richest. The fault-finder will find faults even in paradise. Love your life.

HENRY DAVID THOREAU

The best help is not to bear the troubles of others for them, but to inspire them with courage and energy to bear their burdens for themselves and meet the difficulties of life bravely.

SIR JOHN LUBBOCK

The world is a looking-glass, and gives back to every man the reflection of his own face. Frown at it, and it in turn will look sourly upon you; laugh at it and with it, and it is a jolly, kind companion.

WILLIAM MAKEPEACE THACKERAY

When you get into a tight place and everything goes against you, till it seems as though you could not hold on a minute longer, never give up then, for that is just the place and time that the tide will turn.

HARRIET BEECHER STOWE

IT is by affliction chiefly that the heart of man is purified, and that the thoughts are fixed on a better state. Prosperity, unalloyed and imperfect as it is, has power to intoxicate the imagination, to fix the mind upon the present scene, to produce confidence and elation, and to make him who enjoys affluence and honors forget the hand by which they were bestowed. It is seldom that we are otherwise than by affliction awakened to a sense of our imbecility, or taught to know how little all our acquisitions can conduce to safety or quiet, and how justly we may inscribe to the superintendence of a higher power those blessings which in the wantonness of success we considered as the attainments of our policy and courage.

SAMUEL JOHNSON

EVERY moment of worry weakens the soul for its daily combat.

HENRY WOOD

I LOVE the man that can smile in trouble, that can gather strength from distress, and grow brave by reflection.

THOMAS PAINE

ALL skill ought to be exerted for universal good. Every man has owed much to others and ought to repay the kindness that he has received.

SAMUEL JOHNSON

GREAT minds have purposes; others have wishes. Little minds are tamed and subdued by misfortunes, but great minds rise above them.

WASHINGTON IRVING

ANY one can carry his burden, however hard, until night falls. Anyone can do his work, however hard, for one day.

ROBERT LOUIS STEVENSON

ONLY those who have the patience to do simple things perfectly will acquire the skill to do difficult things easily.

JOHANN FRIEDRICH VON SCHILLER

A HANDFUL of pine-seed will cover mountains with the green majesty of forest. I too will set my face to the wind and throw my handful of seed on high.

WILLIAM SHARP

EVERY man is the builder of the temple called his body — we are all sculptors and painters and our material is our own flesh and blood and bones. Any nobleness begins at once to refine a man's features.

HENRY DAVID THOREAU

SEARCH thy own heart; what paineth thee in others in thyself may be.

JOHN GREENLEAF WHITTIER

IF, when you look into your own heart, you find nothing wrong there, what is there to worry about, what is there to fear?

CONFUCIUS

THE more sympathies we gain or awaken for what is beautiful, by so much deeper will be our sympathy for that which is most beautiful, the human soul.

JAMES RUSSELL LOWELL

THE power which resides in an individual is new in nature, and none but he knows what this is which he can do, nor does he know until he has tried.

RALPH WALDO EMERSON

43

ENDEAVOR to be patient in bearing the defects and infirmities of others, of what sort soever they be; for thou thyself also hast many failings which must be borne with by others.

THOMAS À KEMPIS

MY own experience and development deepen every day my conviction that our moral progress may be measured by the degree in which we sympathize with individual suffering and individual joy.

GEORGE ELIOT

LET joy, temperance and repose
Slam the door on the doctor's nose.

HENRY WADSWORTH LONGFELLOW

PATIENCE is bitter, but its fruit sweet.

JEAN JACQUES ROUSSEAU

SELF-CONFIDENCE is the first requisite to great undertakings.

SAMUEL JOHNSON

PEOPLE do not lack strength; they lack will.

VICTOR HUGO

My heart, which is full to overflowing, has often been solaced and refreshed by music when sick and weary.

MARTIN LUTHER

THERE is ever a song somewhere, my dear,
    Be the skies above dark or fair,
There is ever a song that our hearts may
    hear —
There is ever a song somewhere, my dear,
There is ever a song somewhere!

JAMES WHITCOMB RILEY

WITH every rising of the sun
Think of your life as just begun.

ANONYMOUS

EVERY man's life is a fairy-tale written by God's fingers.

HANS CHRISTIAN ANDERSEN

HE jests at scars that never felt a wound.

WILLIAM SHAKESPEARE

THE greater the obstacle the more glory in overcoming it.

JEAN BAPTISTE MOLIÈRE

46

OUR greatest glory is not in never falling, but in rising every time we fall.

CONFUCIUS

CALL no faith false which e'er hath brought
   Relief to any laden life,
Cessation from the pain of thought,
   Refreshment 'mid the dust of strife.

SIR LEWIS MORRIS

ALL common things, each day's events,
   That with the hour begin and end,
Our pleasures and our discontents,
   Are rounds by which we may ascend.

HENRY WADSWORTH LONGFELLOW

A GAY, serene spirit is the source of all that is noble and good.

JOHANN FRIEDRICH VON SCHILLER

A MOMENT's insight is sometimes worth a life's experience.

OLIVER WENDELL HOLMES

MANY men owe the grandeur of their lives to their tremendous difficulties.

CHARLES HADDON SPURGEON

WE expect to pass through this world but once. Any good we can do, therefore, or any kindness that we can show to any fellow creature, let us do it now; let us not defer or neglect it, for we shall not pass this way again.

STEPHEN GRELLET

YOUTH will never live to age unless they keep themselves in health with exercise, and in heart with joyfulness.

SIR PHILIP SIDNEY

No man can answer for his courage who has never been in danger.

FRANÇOIS, DUC DE LA ROCHEFOUCAULD

IN the harsh face of life, faith can read a bracing gospel.

ROBERT LOUIS STEVENSON

WHERE words fail, music speaks.

HANS CHRISTIAN ANDERSEN

KINDNESS — a language which the dumb can speak, and the deaf can understand.

CHRISTIAN BOVÉE

To endure is greater than to dare; to tire out hostile fortune; to be daunted by no difficulty; to keep heart when all have lost it; to go through intrigue spotless; to forego even ambition when the end is gained — who can say this is not greatness?

WILLIAM MAKEPEACE THACKERAY

WE never know how high we are
    Till we are called to rise;
And then, if we are true to plan,
    Our statures touch the skies.

The heroism we recite
    Would be a daily thing,
Did not ourselves the cubits warp
    For fear to be a king.

EMILY DICKINSON

WHO does not in some sort live to others, does not live much to himself.

MIGUEL DE MONTAIGNE

THERE is a wisdom in this beyond the rules of physic. A man's own observation, what he finds good of and what he finds hurt of, is the best physic to preserve health.

FRANCIS BACON

Owe not thy humility unto humiliation from adversity, but look humbly down in that state when others look upwards upon thee.

SIR THOMAS BROWNE

JOKING and humor are pleasant, and often of extreme utility.

CICERO

'Tis a little thing
To give a cup of water; yet its draught
Of cool refreshment, drained by fevered lips,
May give a shock of pleasure to the frame
More exquisite than when nectarean juice
Renews the life of joy in happiest hours.

SIR THOMAS NOON TALFOURD

Be not afraid to pray; to pray is right.
Pray, if thou canst, with hope, but ever pray,
Though hope be weak, or sick with long
   delay.
Pray in the darkness if there be no light.

HARTLEY COLERIDGE

NONE is so near the gods as he who shows kindness.

SENECA

GREAT people are not affected by each puff of wind that blows ill. Like great ships, they sail serenely on, in a calm sea or a great tempest.

GEORGE WASHINGTON

KING Hassan, well beloved, was wont to say
  When aught went wrong, or any project
    failed:
"Tomorrow, friends, will be another day!"
  And in that faith he slept and so prevailed.

JAMES BUCKHAM

LET nothing disturb thee, nothing affright
    thee;
All things are passing; God never changeth;
Patient endurance attaineth all things;
Who God possesseth in nothing is wanting;
Alone God sufficeth.

HENRY WADSWORTH LONGFELLOW

To work, to help, and to be helped, to learn sympathy through suffering, to learn faith by perplexity, is to reach truth through wonder, behold! — this is what it means to prosper, this is what it is to live.

PHILLIPS BROOKS

AMONG the attributes of God, although they are all equal, mercy shines with even more brilliance than justice.

MIGUEL DE CERVANTES

LET us not say: Every man is the architect of his own fortune; but let us say: Every man is the architect of his own character.

GEORGE DANA BOARDMAN

OCCASIONS do not make a man either strong or weak, but they show what he is.

THOMAS À KEMPIS

HOLD yourself responsible for a higher standard than anybody else expects of you. Never excuse yourself. Never pity yourself. Be a hard taskmaster to yourself — and be lenient with everybody else.

HENRY WARD BEECHER

IDEALS are like stars: You will not succeed in touching them with your hands, but like the seafaring man on the desert of waters, you choose them as your guides, and following them, you reach your destiny.

CARL SCHURZ

FINISH every day and be done with it. You have done what you could; some blunders and absurdities crept in — forget them as soon as you can. Tomorrow is a new day. You shall begin it well and serenely, and with too high a spirit to be encumbered with your old nonsense.

RALPH WALDO EMERSON

Do you wish to be great?
Then begin by being little.
Do you desire to construct a lofty fabric?
Think first about the foundations of humility.
The higher your structure is to be,
The deeper must be its foundation.
Modest humility is beauty's crown.

ST. AUGUSTINE

HE that would live in peace and ease
Must not speak all he knows nor judge
    all he sees.

BENJAMIN FRANKLIN

No soul is desolate as long as there is a human being for whom it can feel trust and reverence.

GEORGE ELIOT

SYMPATHY wanting, all is wanting. — Personal magnetism is the conductor of the sacred spark that puts us in human communion, and gives us to company, conversation, and ourselves.

AMOS BRONSON ALCOTT

DESPAIR of all recovery spoils longevity,
And makes men's miseries of alarming
    brevity.

LORD BYRON

STARS may be seen from the bottom of a deep well, when they cannot be seen from the top of the mountain. So many things are learned in adversity which the prosperous man dreams not of.

CHARLES HADDEN SPURGEON

THIS is the day which the Lord hath made; we will rejoice and be glad in it.

PSALMS 118:24

HOPE awakens courage. He who can implant courage in the human soul is the best physician.

KARL VON KNEBEL

Never attempt to bear more than one kind of trouble at once. Some people bear three kinds — all they have had — all they have now — and all they ever expect to have.

Edward Everett Hale

No one is useless in this world who lightens the burden of it to any one else.

Charles Dickens

Help thy brother's boat across, and lo! thine own has reached the shore.

Hindu Proverb

Patience is but lying to and riding out the gale.

Henry Ward Beecher

The burden becomes light which is cheerfully borne.

Ovid

I will lift up mine eyes unto the hills, from whence cometh my help.

My help cometh from the Lord, which made heaven and earth.

Psalms 121:1, 2

A MAN should never be ashamed to say he has been in the wrong, which is but saying in other words he is wiser today than he was yesterday.

ALEXANDER POPE

WE were put here to do what service we can, for honor and not for hire. . . . The soul of piety was killed long ago by that idea of reward.

ROBERT LOUIS STEVENSON

I AM only one,
But still I am one.
I cannot do everything,
But still I can do something;
And because I cannot do everything
I will not refuse to do the something
    that I can do.

EDWARD EVERETT HALE

LOOK not thou down but up!

ROBERT BROWNING

HE who does not think too much of himself is much more esteemed than he imagines.

JOHANN WOLFGANG VON GOETHE

THERE are compensations: and no outward changes of condition in life can keep the nightingale of its eternal meaning from singing in all sorts of different men's hearts.

WILLIAM JAMES

PRIDE is one chief cause of undue anger.

JONATHAN EDWARDS

IN humility the mind is at rest and peace; patience is her daughter.

ST. FRANCIS OF ASSISI

WHAT part soever you have taken upon you, play that as well as you can and make the best of it.

SIR THOMAS MORE

THE great man is he that does not lose his child's heart.

MENCIUS

A MAN must not complain of his "element," or of his "time," or the like; it is thriftless work doing so. His time is bad; well then, he is there to make it better.

THOMAS CARLYLE

THERE is no debt so heavy to a grateful mind as a debt of kindness unpaid.

LAWRENCE STERNE

A THANKFUL heart is not only the greatest virtue, but the parent of all the other virtues.

CICERO

IF I am right, thy grace impart
   Still in the right to stay;
If I am wrong, O, reach my heart
   To find that better way!

ALEXANDER POPE

I WILL tell you, scholar, I have heard a grave divine say that God has two dwellings, one in heaven and the other in a meek and thankful heart.

IZAAK WALTON

PROSPERITY is no just scale; adversity is the only balance to weigh friends.

PLUTARCH

ADOPT the pace of nature: her secret is patience.

RALPH WALDO EMERSON

MEN's habitual words and acts imply the idea that they are at liberty to treat their bodies as they please. Disorders entailed by disobedience to Nature's dictates, they regard simply as grievances; not as the effects more or less flagitious.

HERBERT SPENCER

I BEG you take courage; the brave soul can mend even disaster.

CATHERINE OF RUSSIA

IF there were dreams to sell,
    What would you buy?
Some cost a passing bell;
    Some a light sigh
That shakes from Life's fresh crown
Only a rose leaf down.
If there were dreams to sell,
Merry and sad to tell,
And the crier rang the bell,
    What would you buy?

THOMAS LOVELL BEDDOES

LIFE is always worth living, if one have responsive sensibilities.

WILLIAM JAMES

How ridiculous and what a stranger he is who is surprised at anything which happens in life.

MARCUS AURELIUS

. . . POWERFUL grace that lies
In herbs, plants, stones, and their qualities:
For naught so vile that on the earth doth live
But to the earth some special food doth give.

WILLIAM SHAKESPEARE

No radiant pearl which crested Fortune
  wears,
No gem that twinkling hangs from Beauty's
  ears,
Not the bright stars which Night's blue arch
  adorn,
Nor rising suns that gild the vernal morn,
Shine with such lustre as the tear that flows
Down virtue's manly cheek for others' woes.

ERASMUS DARWIN

OUR sympathy is never very deep unless founded on our own feelings. — We pity, but do not enter into the grief which we have never felt.

LETITIA ELIZABETH LANDON

How can I know what I think
until I can see what I say.

Alice in
Wonderland